THE NEW HISTORY OF SHAKESPEARE IN OREGON

By

Daniel DeRoux

Copyright © 2017 Daniel DeRoux

All rights reserved.

ISBN:**1974396908**
ISBN-13: **978-1974396900**

Dedicated to JoAnn
Thank you for loving me.

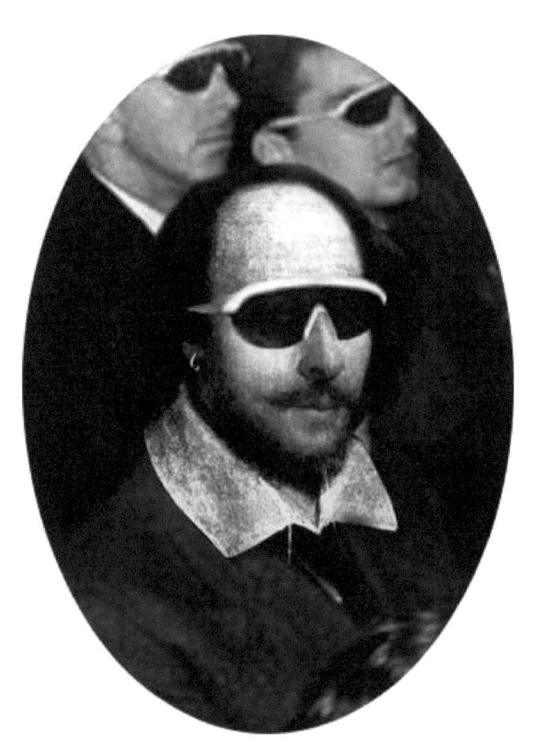

I would like to thank the Ashland and Medford Public Libraries,
The Rogue Valley Historical Society, Omar's Restaurant, and
the Modern Fan Company…stay cool.

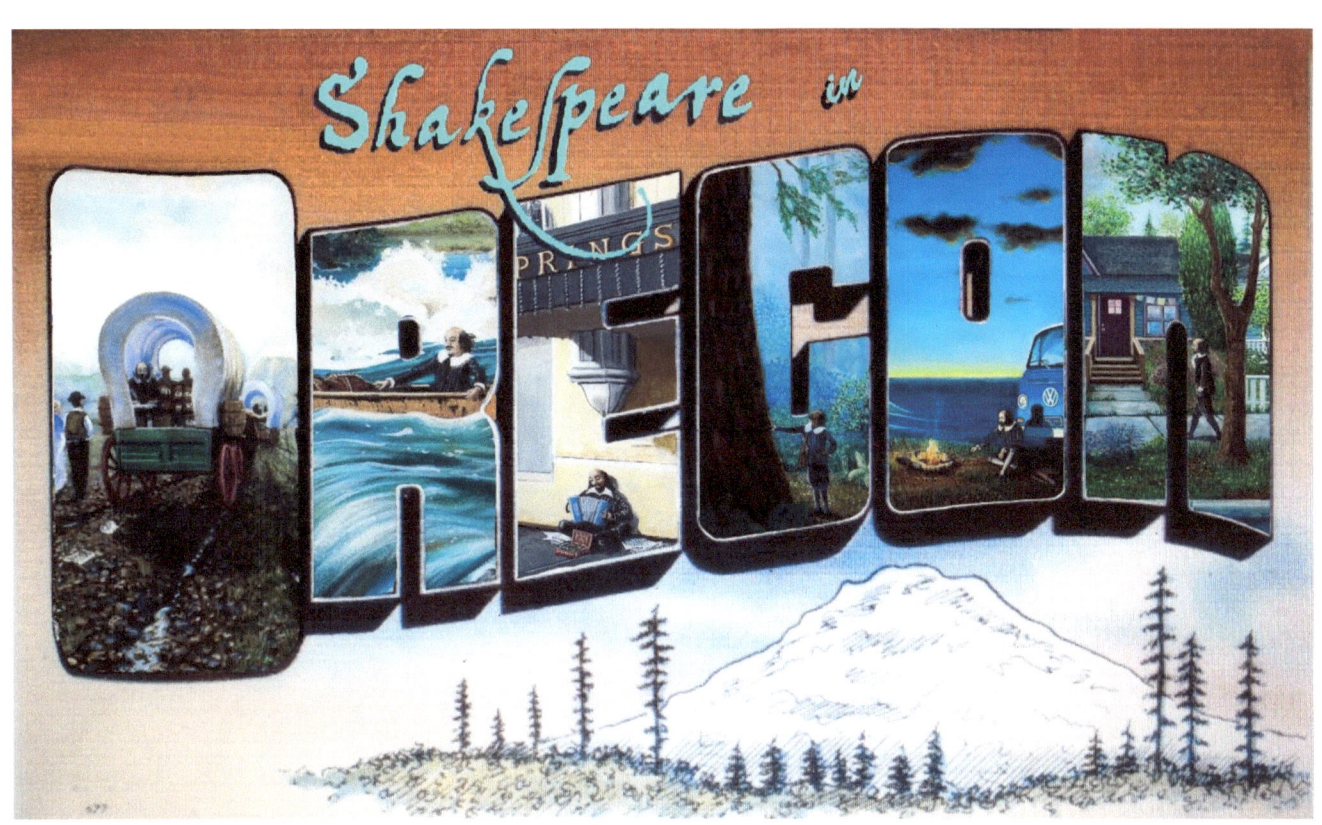

Shakespeare came across the Atlantic in 1850, then across the Oregon Trail.
He has been here for years. Really, he lives just down the street from me.
A lot of people question if William Shakespeare ever existed at all.
They say there are no records of him…no documents…no trace.
Well, it appears they didn't look very hard. I found a lot of things.

At the time of the first publication of this book, the most significant item was probably the photograph of him in the Ashland Plaza around 1920. I looked through piles of photographs looking for that one face, and there it was. You just have to pay attention. And now at this printing, I have two, maybe three photographs of him! He could be in plain sight and no one sees him.
I found a hotel registry, a few grocery receipts, you just have to look.

I've never told anyone before, but 2 years ago as my wife JoAnn and I were walking upstairs to the Black Sheep Pub, Shakespeare, probably in his late 20's, was coming down the stairs with his girlfriend.
No kidding. JoAnn saw him too.
He looked at me like, "Hey old man", and I thought, "There is William Shakespeare!"
I could have reached out and touched his velvet tunic…and then – gone, but not really.
One thing I noticed about this book is that on both of the ship passenger manifests,
which are 70 years apart, his age is given as 25.
I can't explain that…..I don't think anyone can,
but every fact is true.

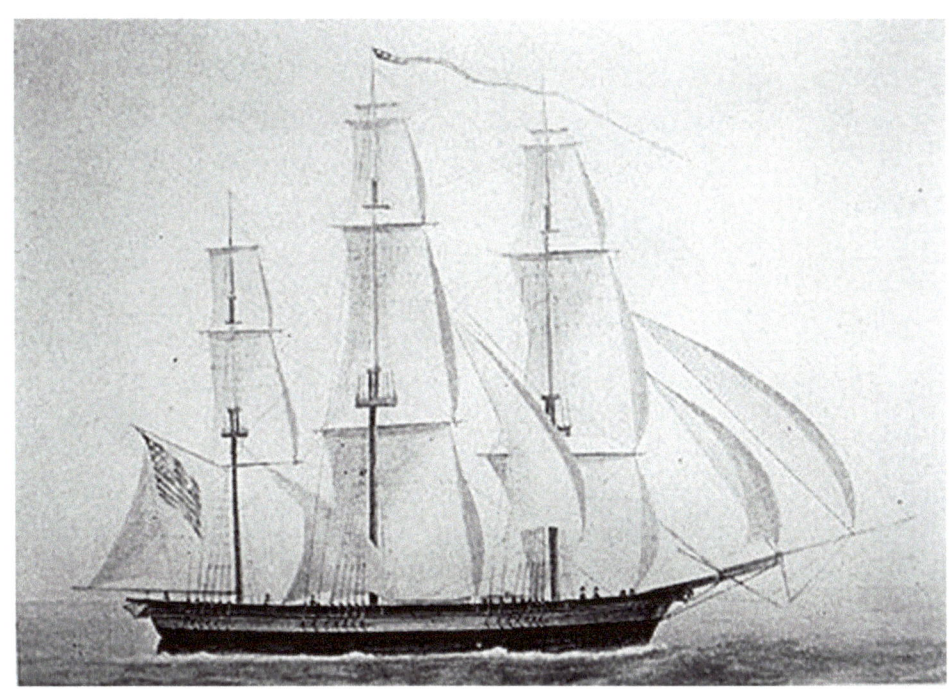

Sailing ship Perseverance

Passenger manifest for the Perseverance
sailing from Plymouth in 1850. All from Germany, except one from England.

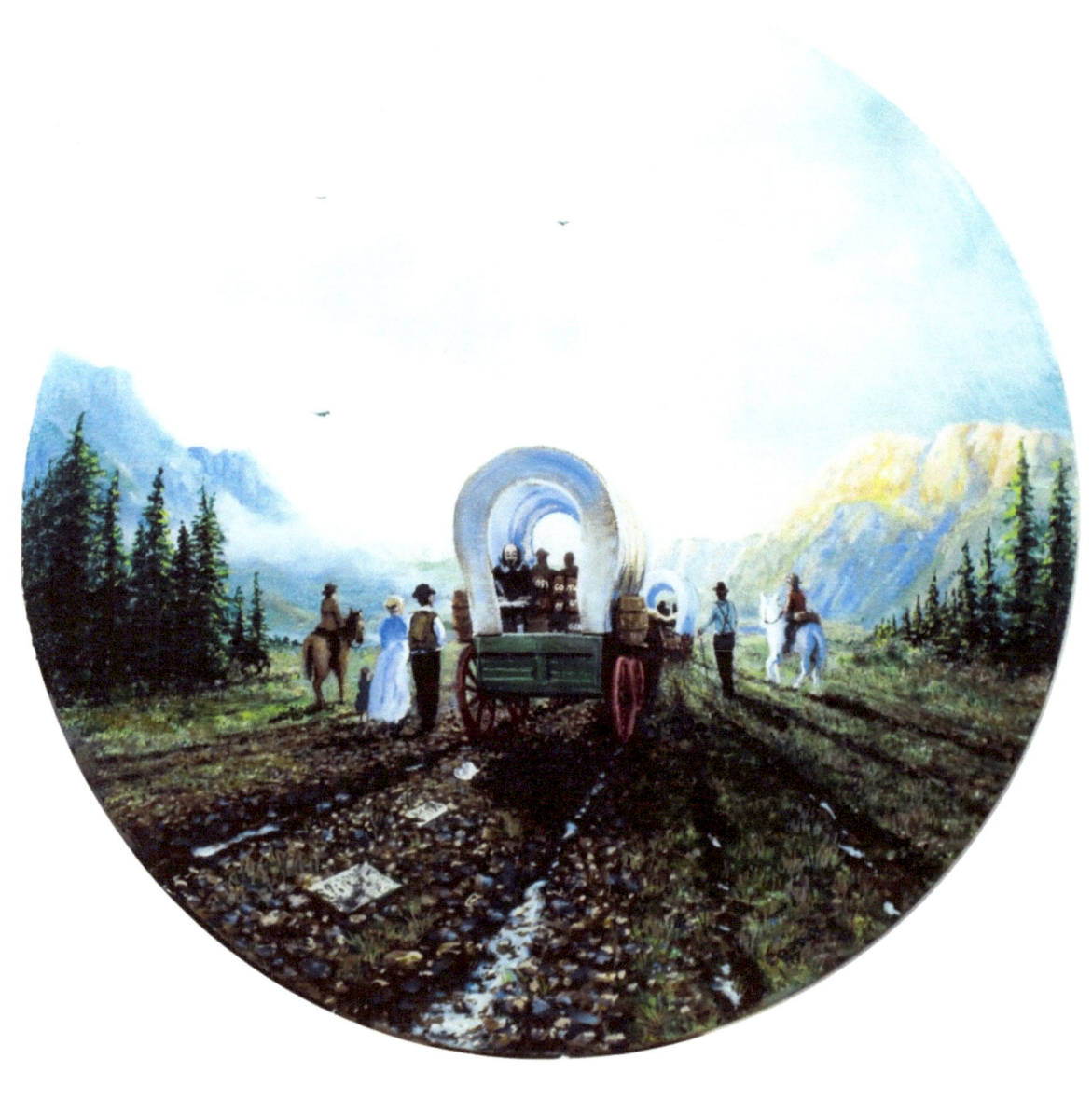

"Dear Mother, I bought a team of oxen and a wagon.
I am headed to Oregon. They have no sales tax."

As Depicted in this painting "Dear Mother…"
the promise of "No Sales Tax" was the magnet
that drew Americans westward to the Oregon Territory.
Life in the Wild West was no place for sissies.
Though Shakespeare was no sissy, a dandy in tights and
pantaloons had a difficult time fitting in.
His quick wit surely must have
saved his life countless times.
Here you can barely see the labels on the crates:
"Costumes" "Props" and "Gin".

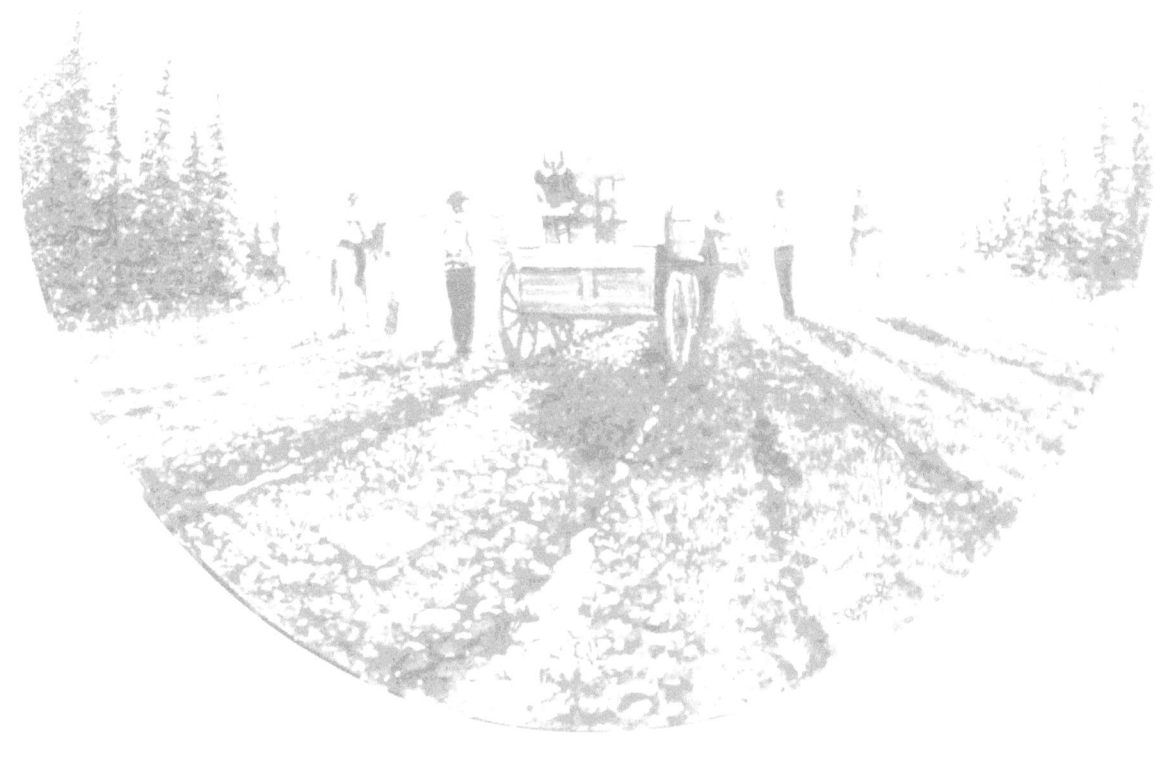

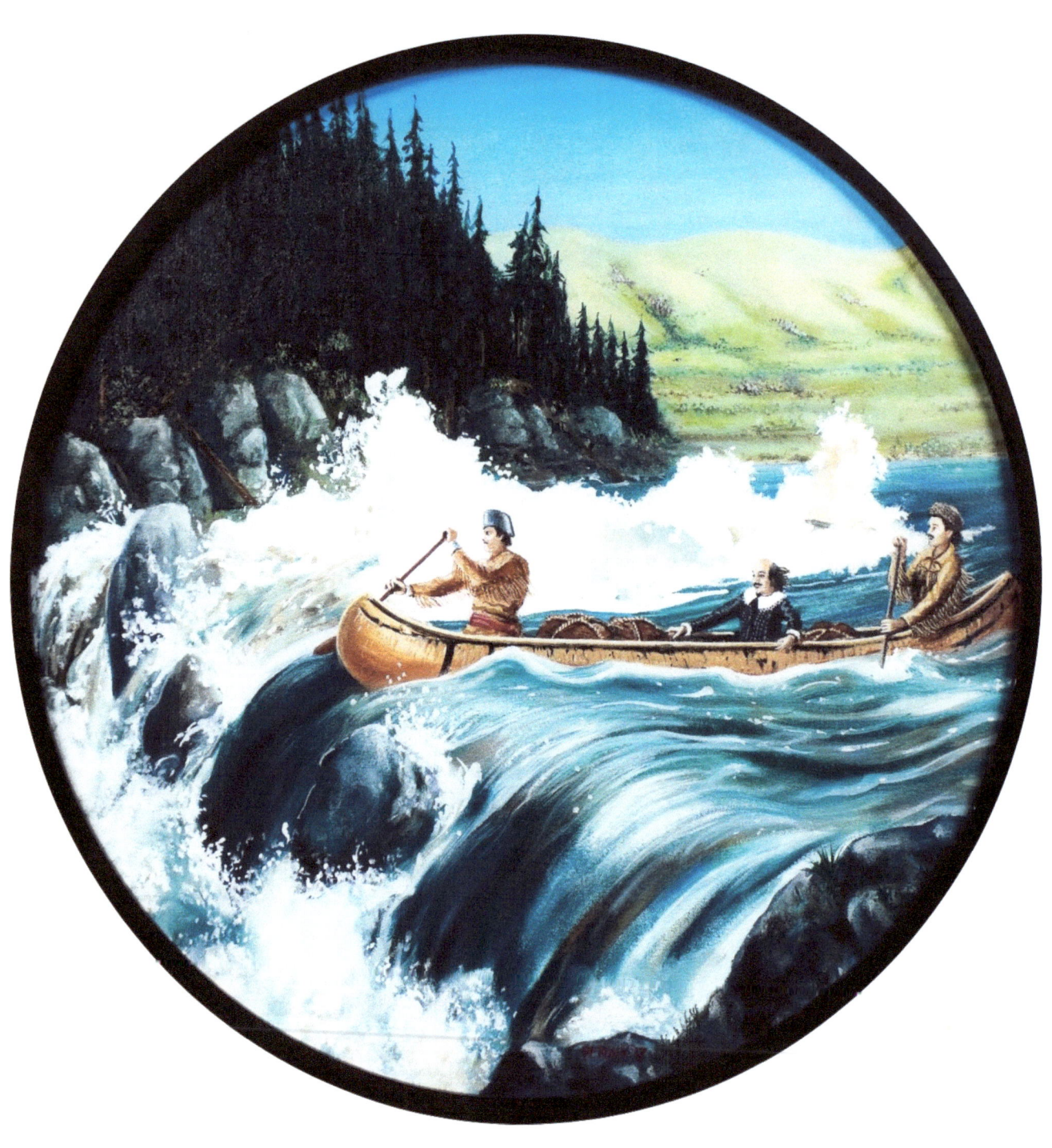

"Cililo Falls"

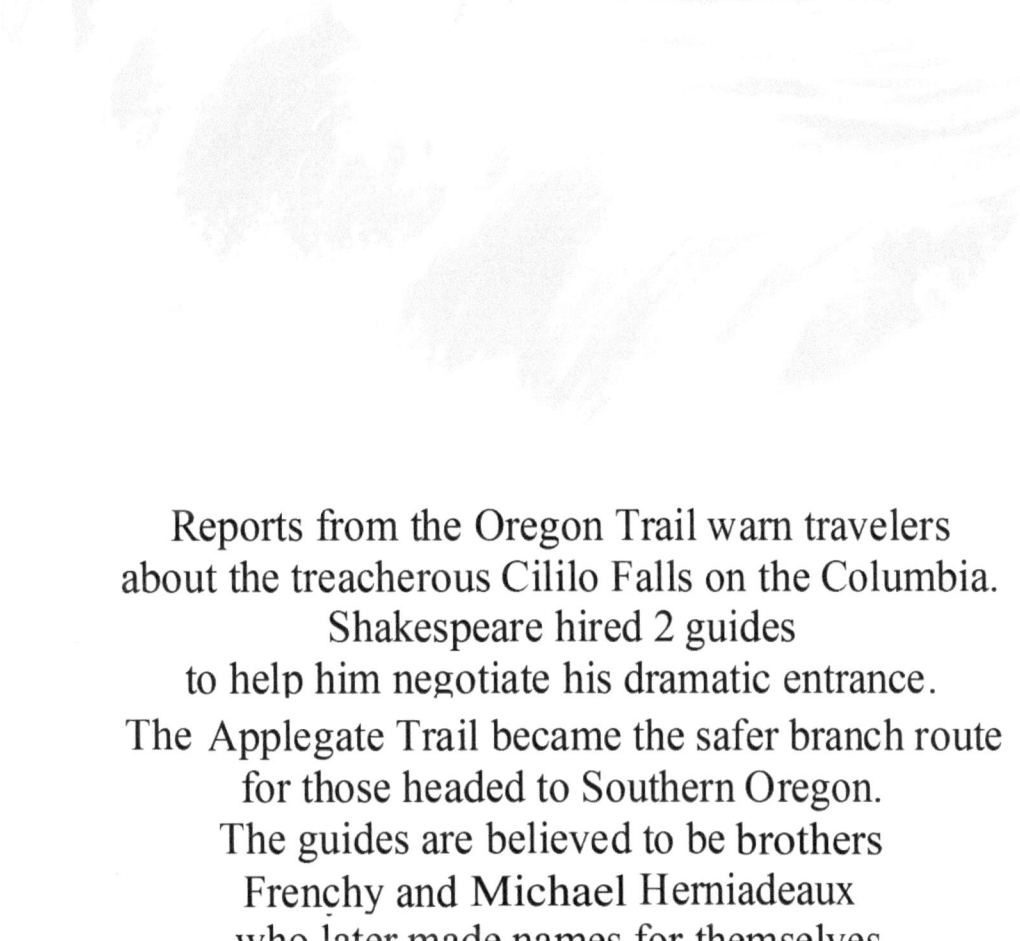

Reports from the Oregon Trail warn travelers
about the treacherous Cililo Falls on the Columbia.
Shakespeare hired 2 guides
to help him negotiate his dramatic entrance.
The Applegate Trail became the safer branch route
for those headed to Southern Oregon.
The guides are believed to be brothers
Frenchy and Michael Herniadeaux
who later made names for themselves.

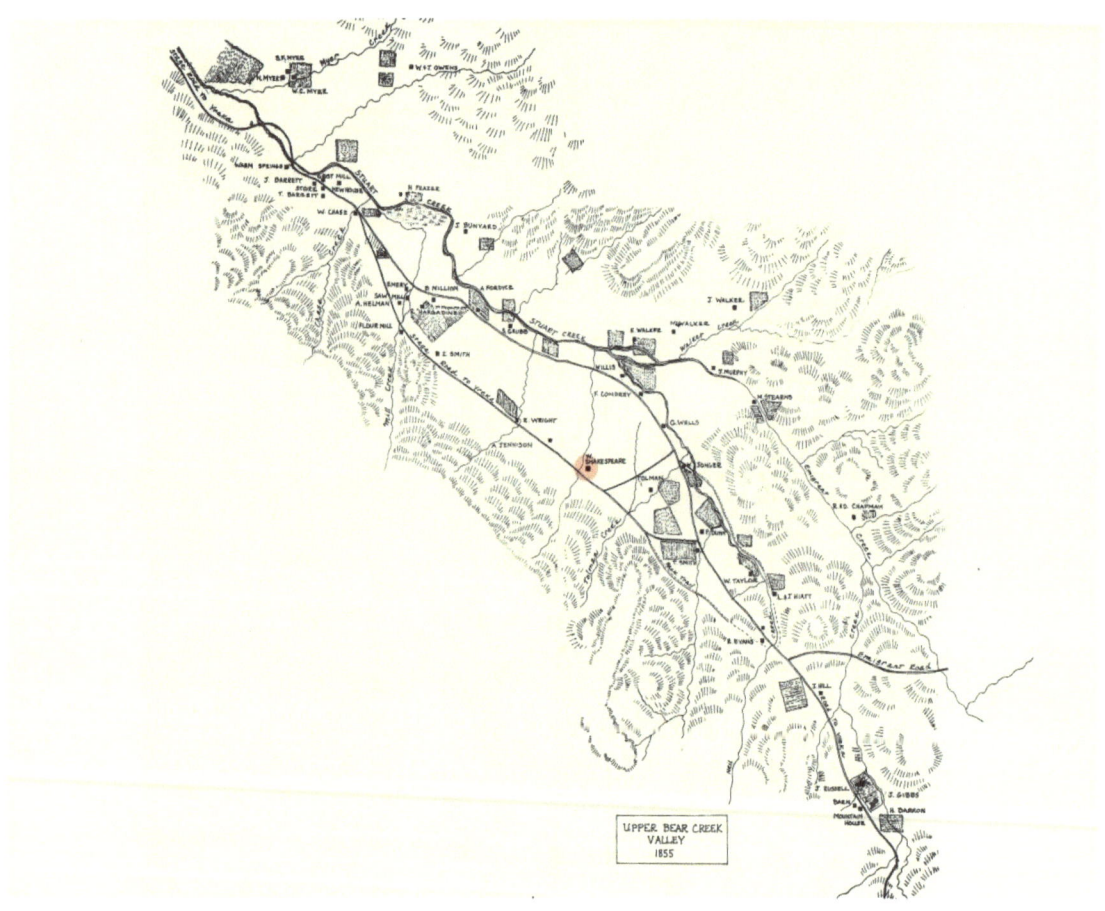

This early map of the Bear Creek Valley (Ashland) from 1855. Clearly shows the residence of Wm. Shakespeare highlighted in red.

THEO. H. LIEBE & CO.,
OREGON STEAM BAKERY,
27 and 29 Pine St. Portland, Or.

Postoffice Box No. 229.

Portland, Or., Aug 24 1886

M_ Nickeyure _ Ashland_

Bought of **THEO. H. LIEBE & CO.**

MANUFACTURERS OF

Fancy Biscuits, Crackers, Bread, Pastry and Ship Bread.

Factory, G and East Park Sts.   No. 27 and 29 PINE STREET, near First.

Terms: Interest charged after maturity.

All bills not remitted for promptly when due, are subject to draft. All claims to be made within THREE days after receipt of goods. No Exchange or Expressage allowed.

Sole Agents for the Celebrated "BOOGE" SUGAR CURED HAMS.

Portland, Oregon, Aug 24   1886

M_ Nickeyure _ Ashland_

Bought of **Mason, Ehrman & Co.**

IMPORTERS, WHOLESALE GROCERS AND COMMISSION MERCHANTS.

Terms: Payable in U. S. Gold Coin. Interest charged after maturity at 10 per cent. per annum.

Nos. 2 & 4 NORTH FRONT STREET.   NEW YORK OFFICE: 112 WALL ST.

N.B.—We do not insure delivery or safe carriage of goods. We ship and take receipts "in good order" and they are at your risk after such receipt is signed by Transportation Co.

| ✓ | 1 | 6 dos T Sugar | 27¾ 254 | 15 | 88 |

All bills not remitted for promptly when due, are subject to draft. All claims to be made within THREE days after receipt of goods. No Exchange or Expressage allowed.

Sole Agents for the Celebrated "BOOGE" SUGAR CURED HAMS.

Portland, Oregon, Aug 24   1886

M_ Nickeyure _

Bought of **Mason, Ehrman & Co.**

IMPORTERS, WHOLESALE GROCERS AND COMMISSION MERCHANTS.

Terms: Payable in U. S. Gold Coin. Interest charged after maturity at 10 per cent. per annum.

Nos. 2 & 4 NORTH FRONT STREET.   NEW YORK OFFICE: 112 WALL ST.

N.B.—We do not insure delivery or safe carriage of goods. We ship and take receipts "in good order" and they are at your risk after such receipt is signed by Transportation Co.

1	For X Salt	100	17	4	25
1¼	" "	500	18	22	50
1½	" Stock "	100	6	9	
				5	575

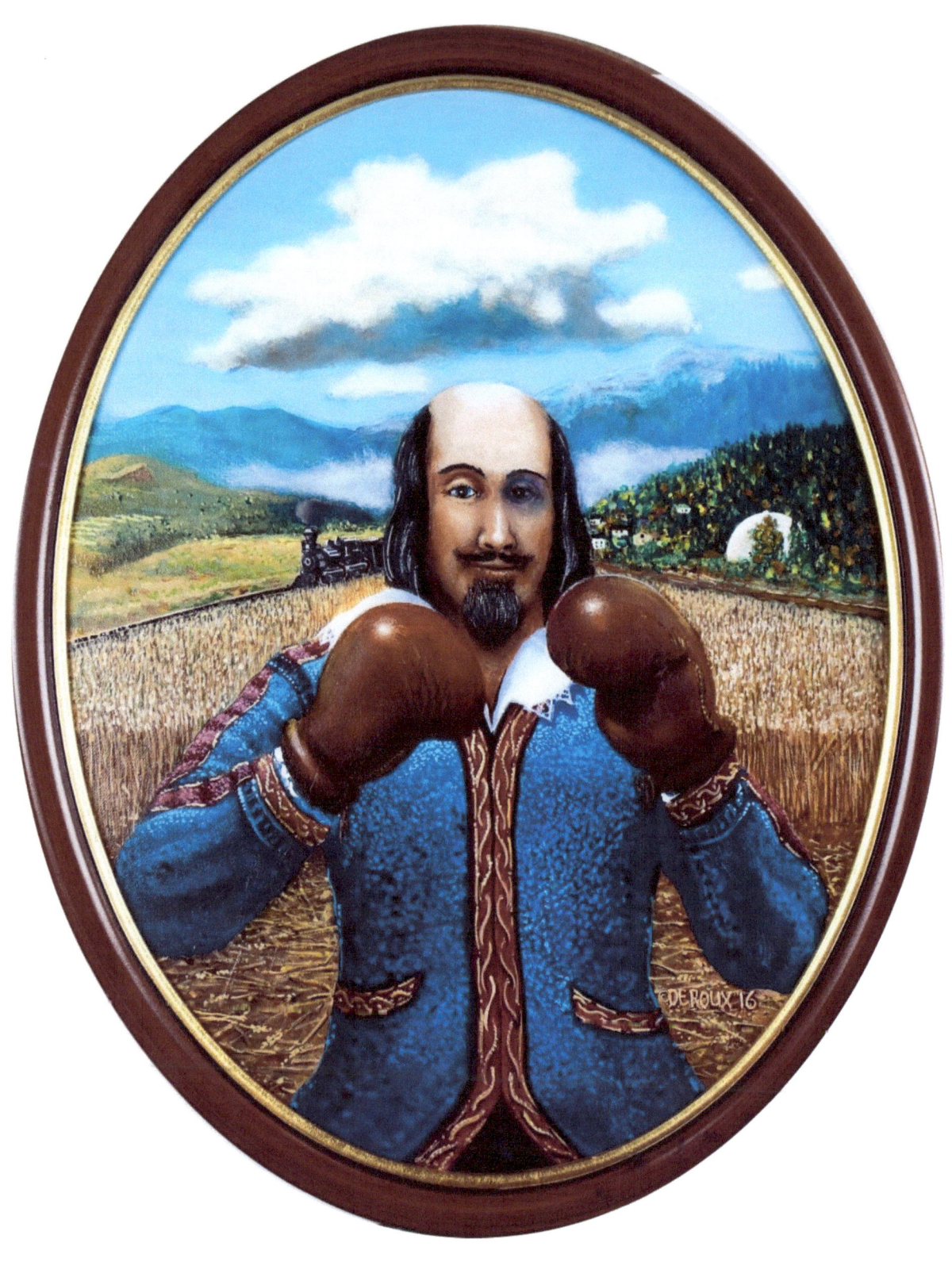

"The Pugilist"

The Chautauqua was a major social, cultural establishment in early Ashland, hosting civic rallies, dances, speeches, concerts, etc.. It was the second largest unsupported domed structure in the country. When it fell to ruin, the foundation wall provided a theatrical setting for the first Shakespearian presentations. The readings were curiously interspersed with bouts of fisticuffs as a money making scheme. Theater and boxing…what were they thinking? Would you pair tennis with chess? Why not bullfighting and maybe roller skating? They were creative, desperate times.

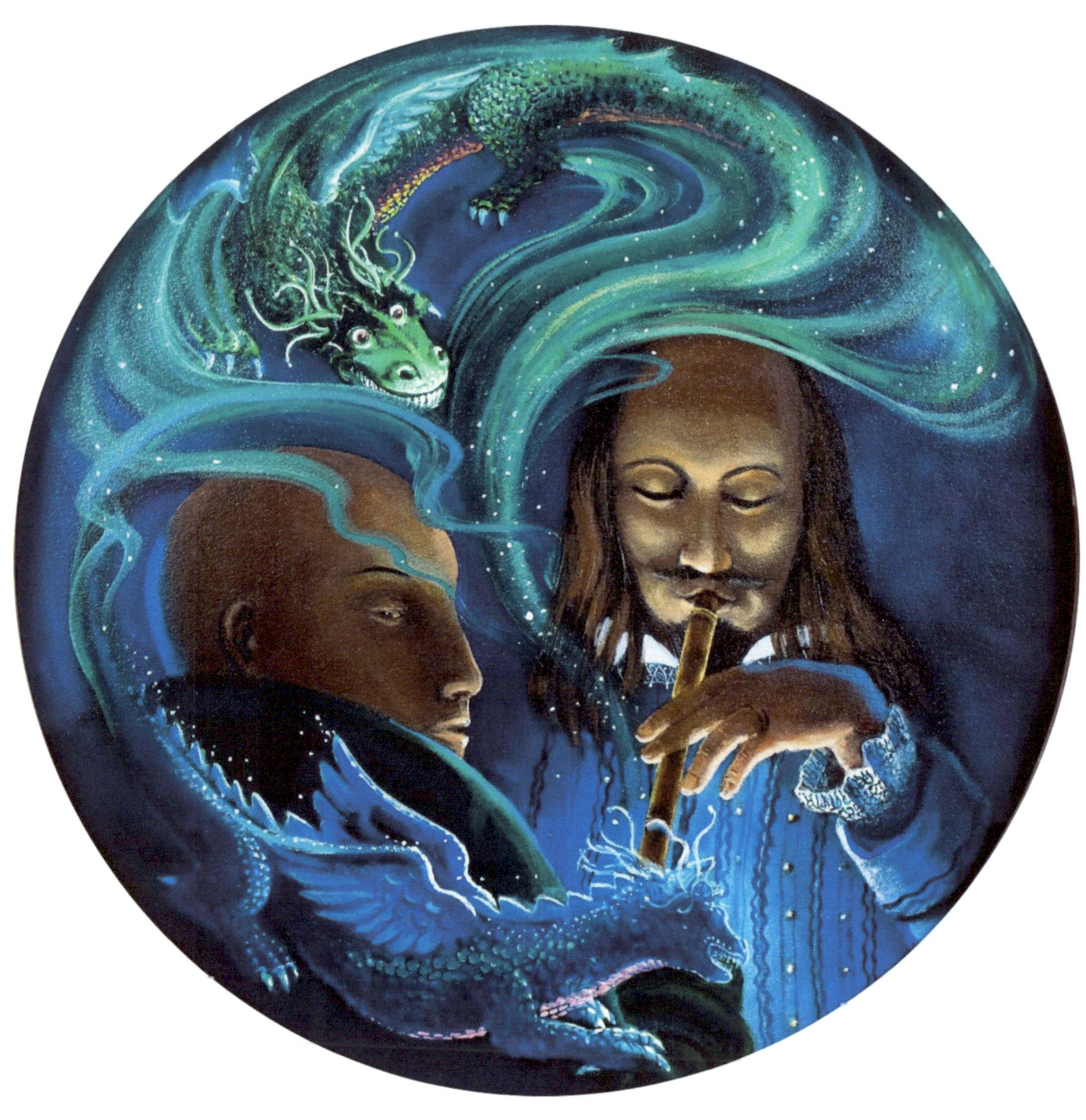

"Chasing the Dragon" became a popular pastime with the laborers in Ashland's Railroad District.

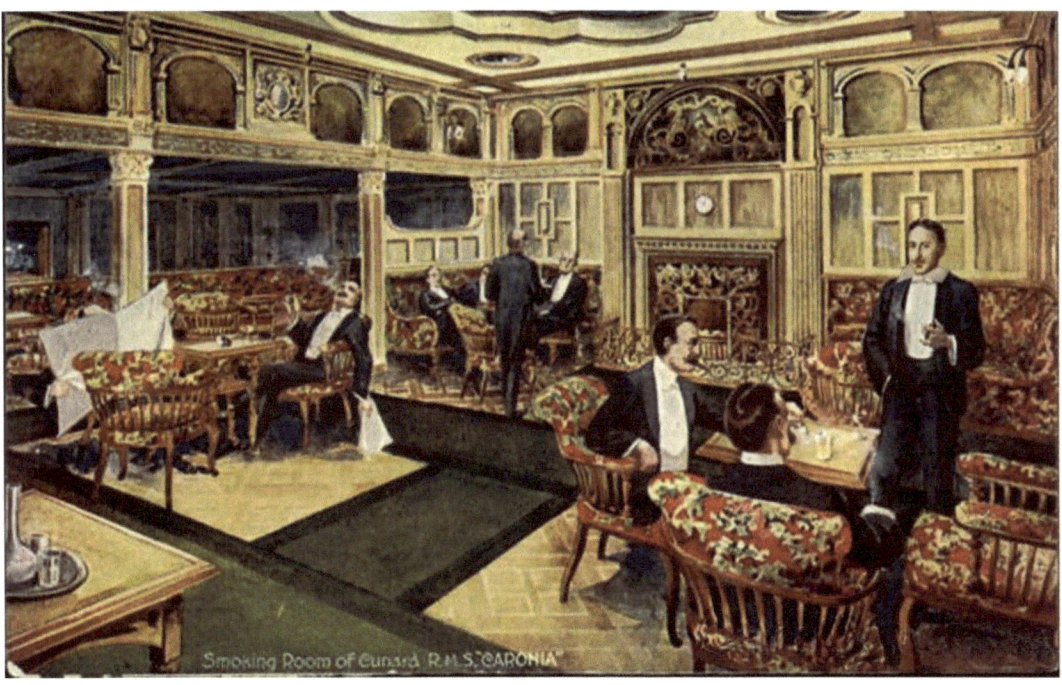

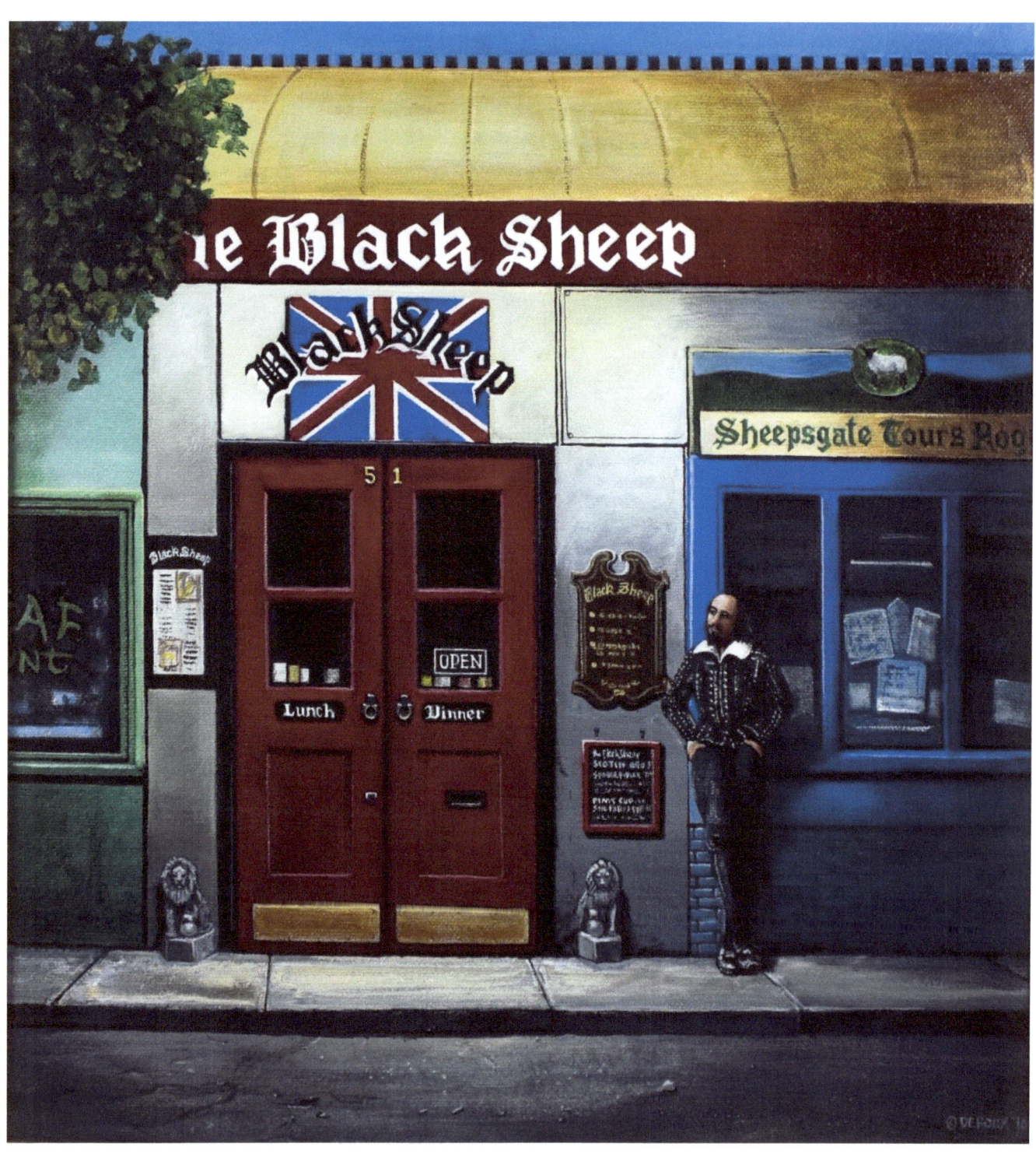

"The Black Sheep"

The International Order of the Odd Fellows
It's home away from home... The Black Sheep...
Many of his days have been spent gazing down from it's windows
to the plaza... a few hours pondering life's rich tapestry
and you have the makings for a Black Sheep:

4 parts gin
1 part molasses
muddled mint

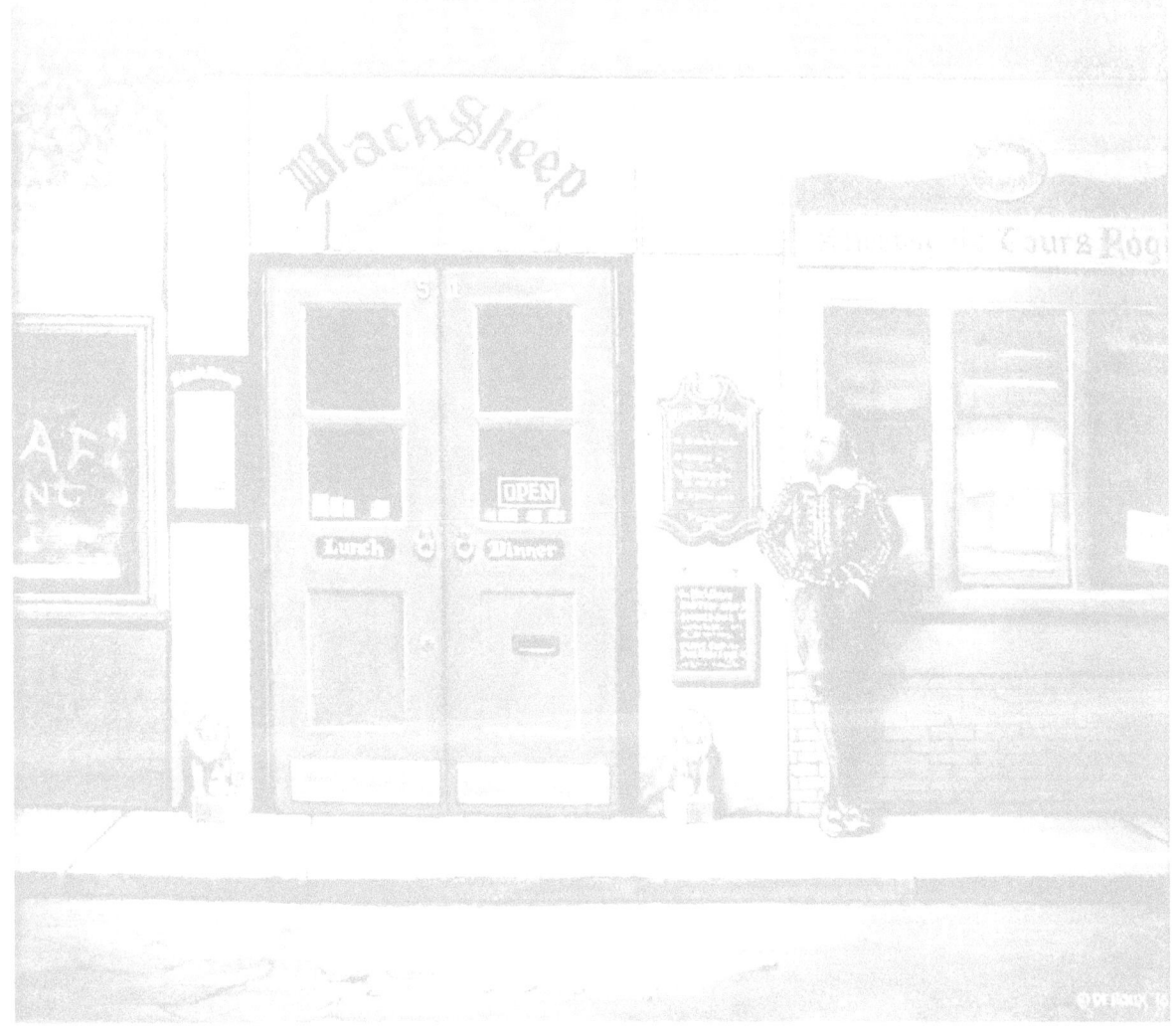

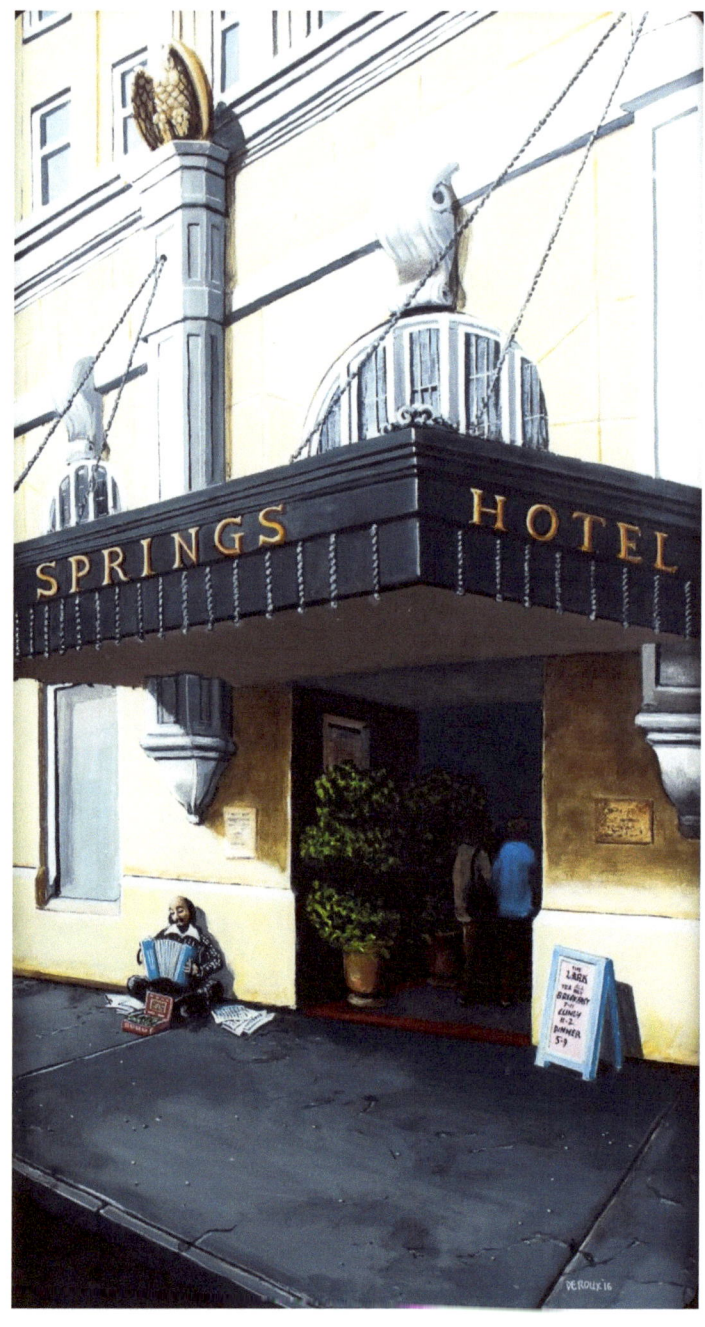

"The Busker"

A good busker can make twice
the income of an average playwright…
on a good day.
Ashland's laws provide for the freedom
to play music on the streets.
Police are trained in musical theory and playing out of
key is allowed only if it is jazz, however jazz is not
allowed in many of the parks.

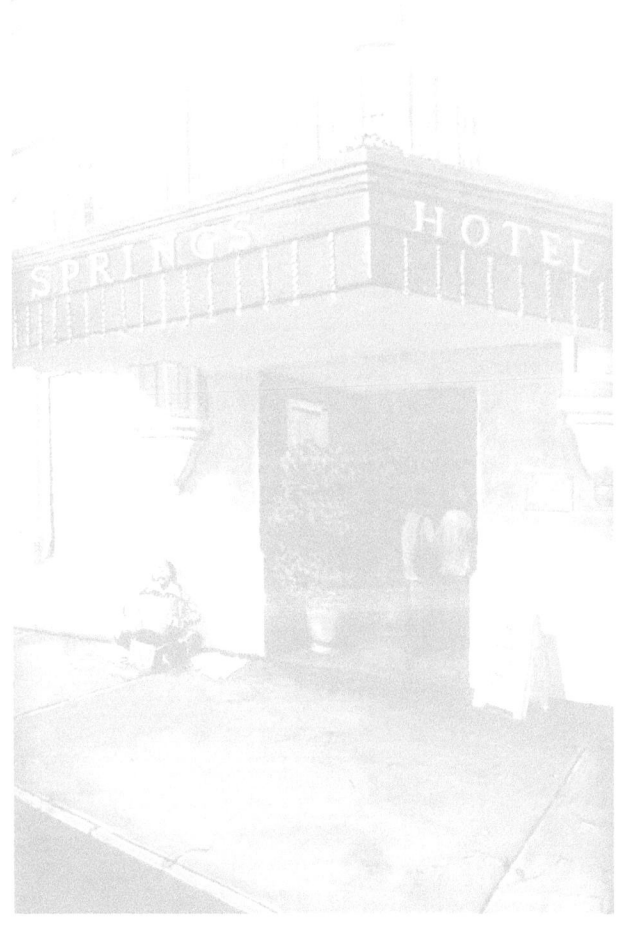

Ashland Tidings
Semi-Weekly
Established 1876.

Issued Mondays and Thursdays

F. D. WAGNER, Publisher and Prop.

Subscription Rates:
One Year ... $2.00
Six Months ... 1.00
Three Months ... .50

Payable in Advance.

Ashland, Or., Thursday, Jan. 14, '09.

GREAT HOUSE-CLEANING SALE!

We request you to pay us a visit during this Clearance Sale. In order to reduce my stock to make room for New Spring Goods, I am offering some exceptional values in Ladies' Suits, Skirts and Coats, Children's Coats, Ladies' Outing Gowns, Ladies' and Children's Shoes, Men's, Ladies' and Children's Underwear, Boys' Clothing, Men's Sweaters, and Men's Night Shirts.

Your inspection of these goods will convince you that we are offering unequalled values in all of these lines if quality is taken into consideration.

1-4 to 1-2 OFF! C. H. VAUPEL
OUR MOTTO: Best Goods at Lowest Prices

STAR THEATRE
PROGRAM FOR THURSDAY, FRIDAY AND SATURDAY.

William Shakespeare's New Play

Pain and Bluster

plus
- Lew Dockstader in Minstrel Mishaps.
- Illustrated Song
- When Jack Comes Sailing Home

First Show Commences ... 7:30
Second ... 8:30
Admission 10 cents.
Corner Main and Second streets.
TOSTEVIN & NELSON, Props.

Real Estate!

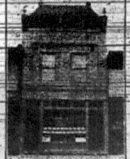

If You Want a Bargain in City Property, Call at this Office

Here are a Few of Them

7-room house with bath and pantry, electric light, sewered and every modern convenience. Large barn, fruits. Fine location near school. $3250, worth $3500

For a cheap place here is a 5-room house; sewer connections; large lot and good variety of fruits; one block from High school. $910, worth $1220.

10 acres of the best red soil, well located; might consider in trade for house and lot in good location.

7-room plastered house, store room, wood house, barn, etc. About 1½ acres of land. $1200.

Only two lots left in the Boulevard Park Addition. $10 cash and $10 per month to close them out. Price only $350. About 20 bearing fruit trees in each lot.

Houses for sale in all parts of the city. Call and look over my list before buying.

Yours truly,
SUSIE L. ALLEN
Phone 362.

CLASSIFIED ADVERTISEMENTS

MISCELLANEOUS

PASTURE FOR HORSES AND COWS
— Horses $3 per month, cows $1.50, 3 miles south of Ashland on main road, old Wells ranch. A. S. Filson, Phone Suburban 39x10.

FOR SALE

FOR SALE—A well broken, gentle young mule. E. T. Staples, Hotel Oregon.

FOR SALE—Lumber. Apply at Commercial Club—or E. T. Staples.

FOR SALE—My property on Granite street...

ORNAMENTAL HEDGE PLANTS—Small fruits, lawn shrubbery, shade trees, evergreens. Now is the time to order pain trees for spring delivery. See me before ordering. Wm. Nelson, 792 B street, Ashland.

ENGLISH WOLF HOUNDS—Six puppies now three months old for sale; best strain in United States; hunting dogs and coyote exterminators. For terms apply to or address J. B. Herrin, Ashland.

ACETYLENE GAS PLANT—For sale in good condition. See C. E. Lane.

JUST A MOMENT!

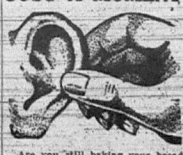

Are you still baking your own bread? Still enduring all that needless drudgery? Just order today some of our product and note the genuine wholesomeness, purity and unsurpassed flavor—and that makes up your mind whether or not you're going to break down your health baking.

A trial solicited

Vienna Bakery
E. E. MILLER, Prop.
Phone 301. 29 Main St.

NOW ON HAND, FOR INSPECTION, SALE AND DELIVERY

10,000 Fruit Trees

All standard varieties of Apples, Pears, Cherries, Peaches, Almonds, Prunes, and many other varieties of Nursery Stock. Plenty of NEWTOWN Apples.

T. H. THOMPSON'S ASHLAND NURSERY
143 GRANITE STREET

WOOD For Sale
Phone 686

YARDS: 2d and B Sts.
Ashland, Ore.

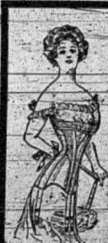

The Racket Store

THIS LADY wishes to call attention not so much to B. & G. Corsets as to HOLIDAY GOODS. There is something for all—Dolls, Drums, Books, Cotton, Linen and Silk Handkerchiefs, Children's Rocking Chairs, Beautiful Stationery, Boxes, Purses, and things too numerous to mention.

C. F. MILLS & CO.

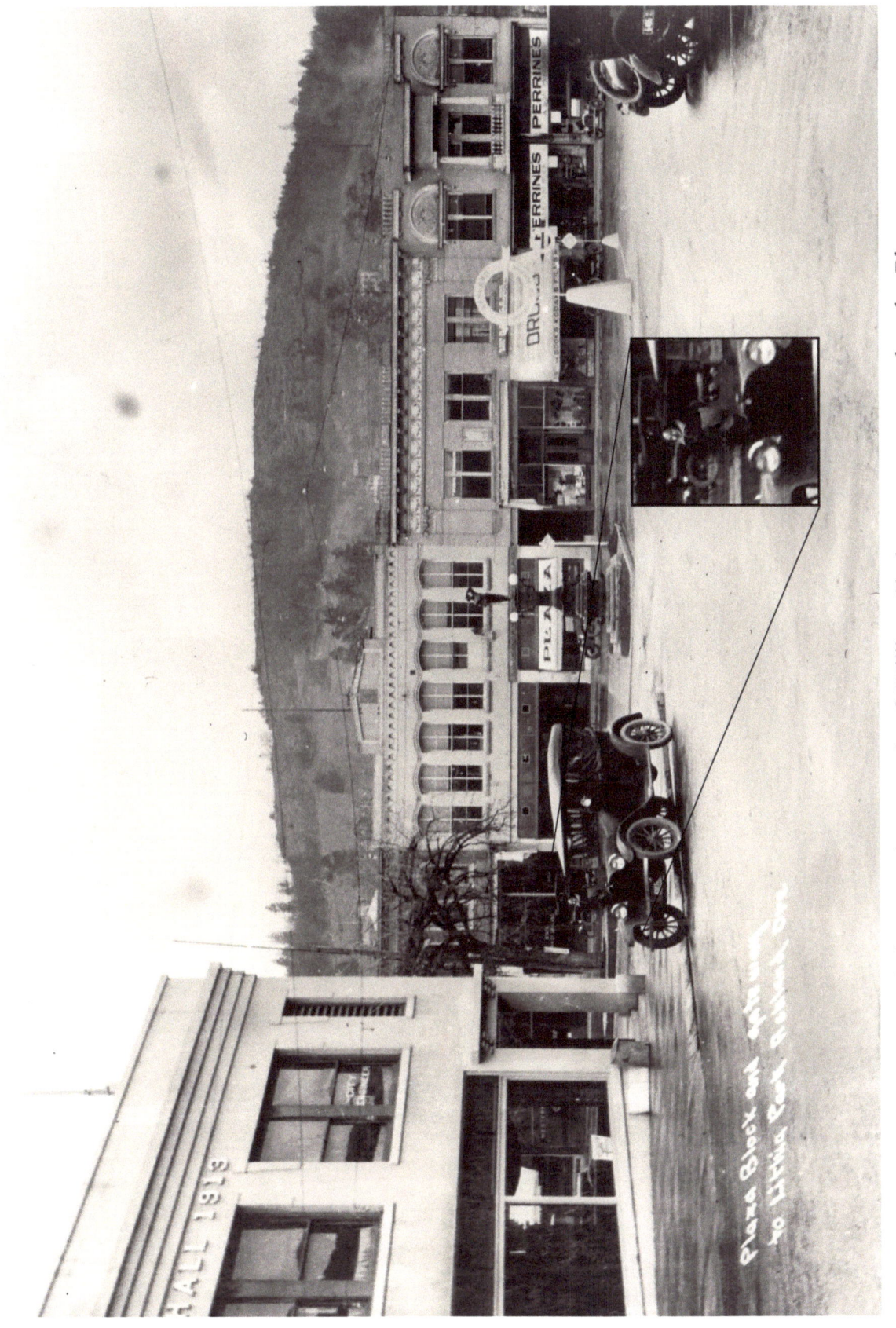

The only known photograph of William Shakespeare, captured at the Plaza

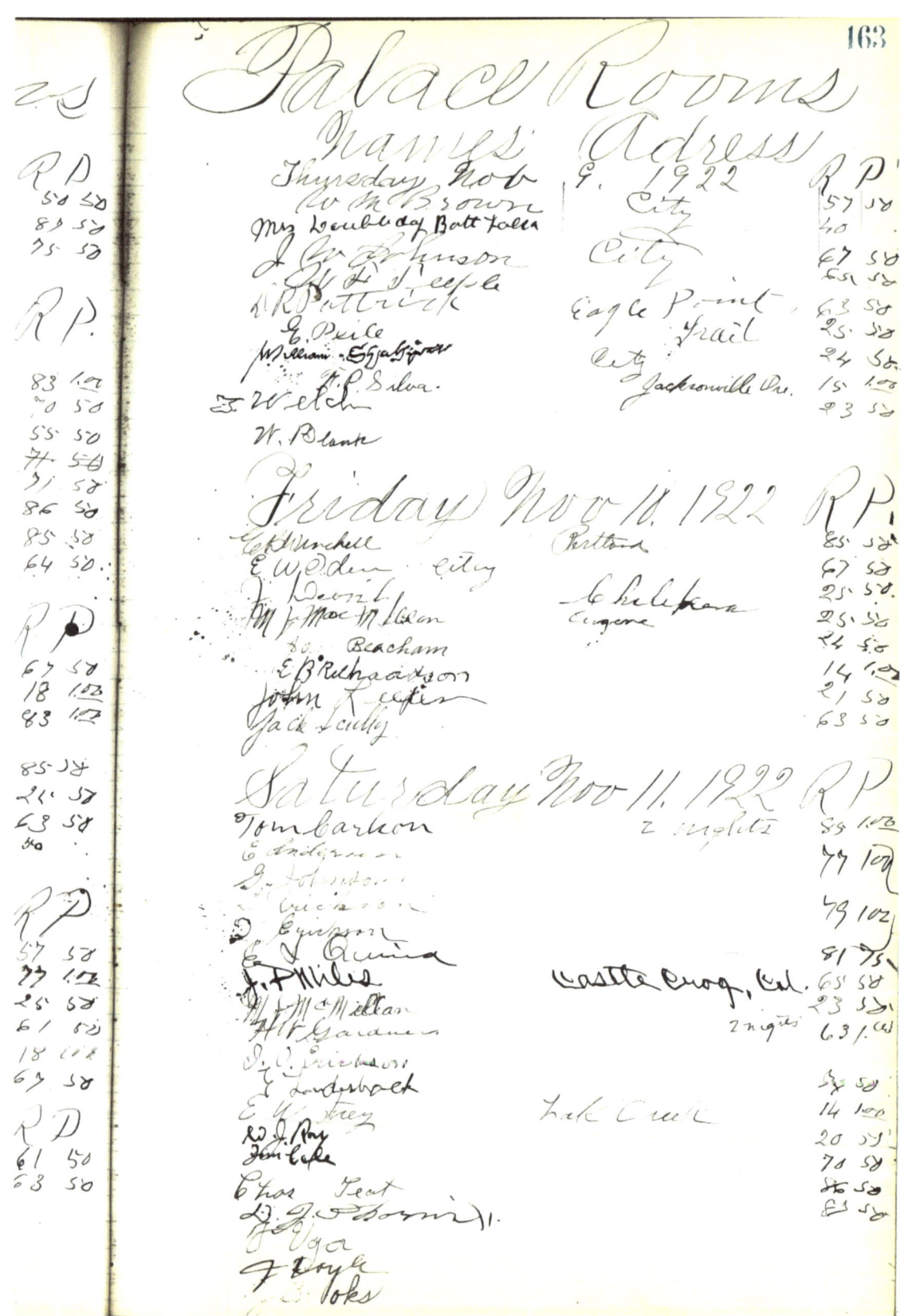

**Nov. 9, 1922, Palace Rooms, Medford.
The ink splattered in row #7 is Shakespeare's signature.**

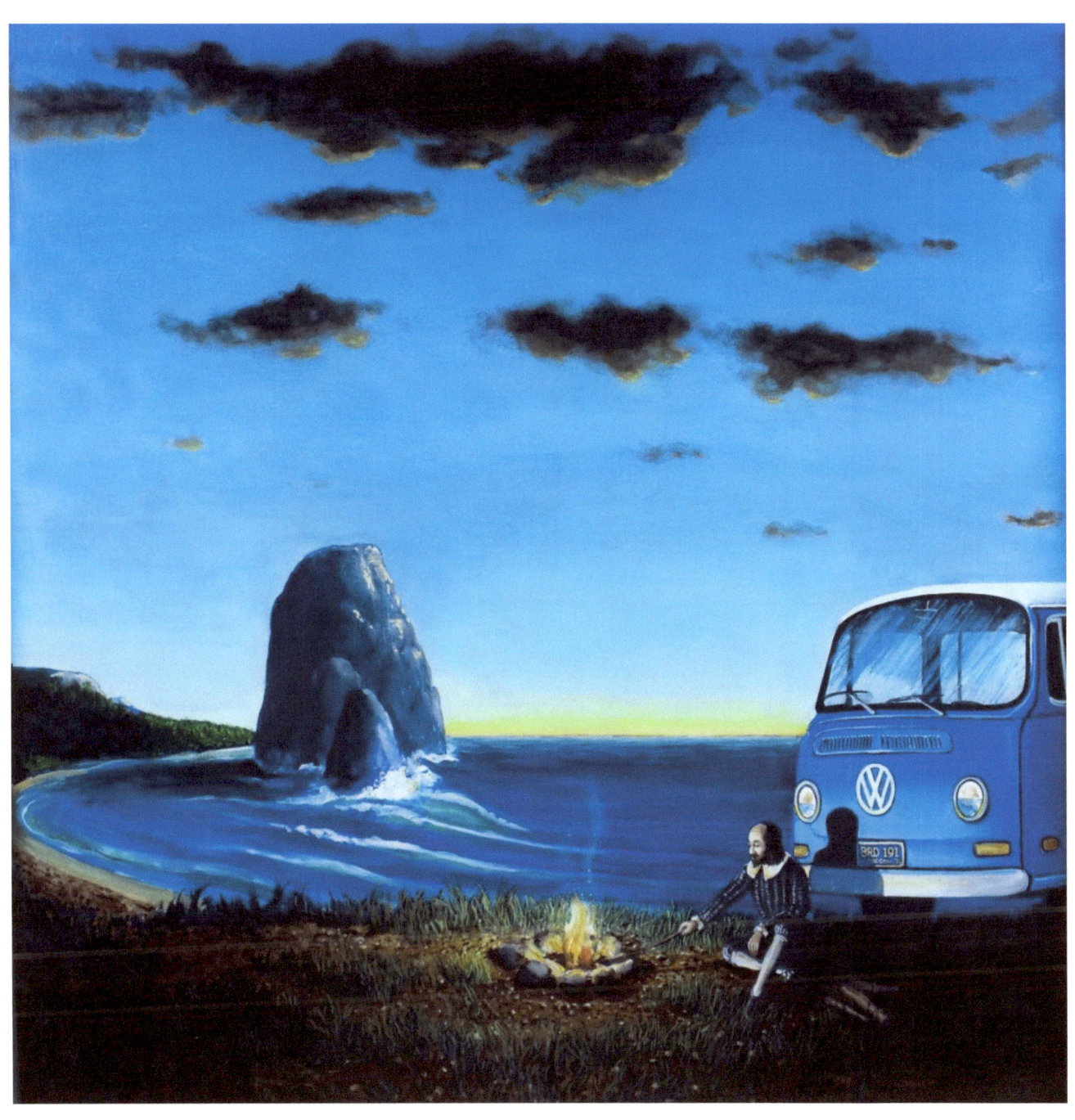

"Getting Clear"

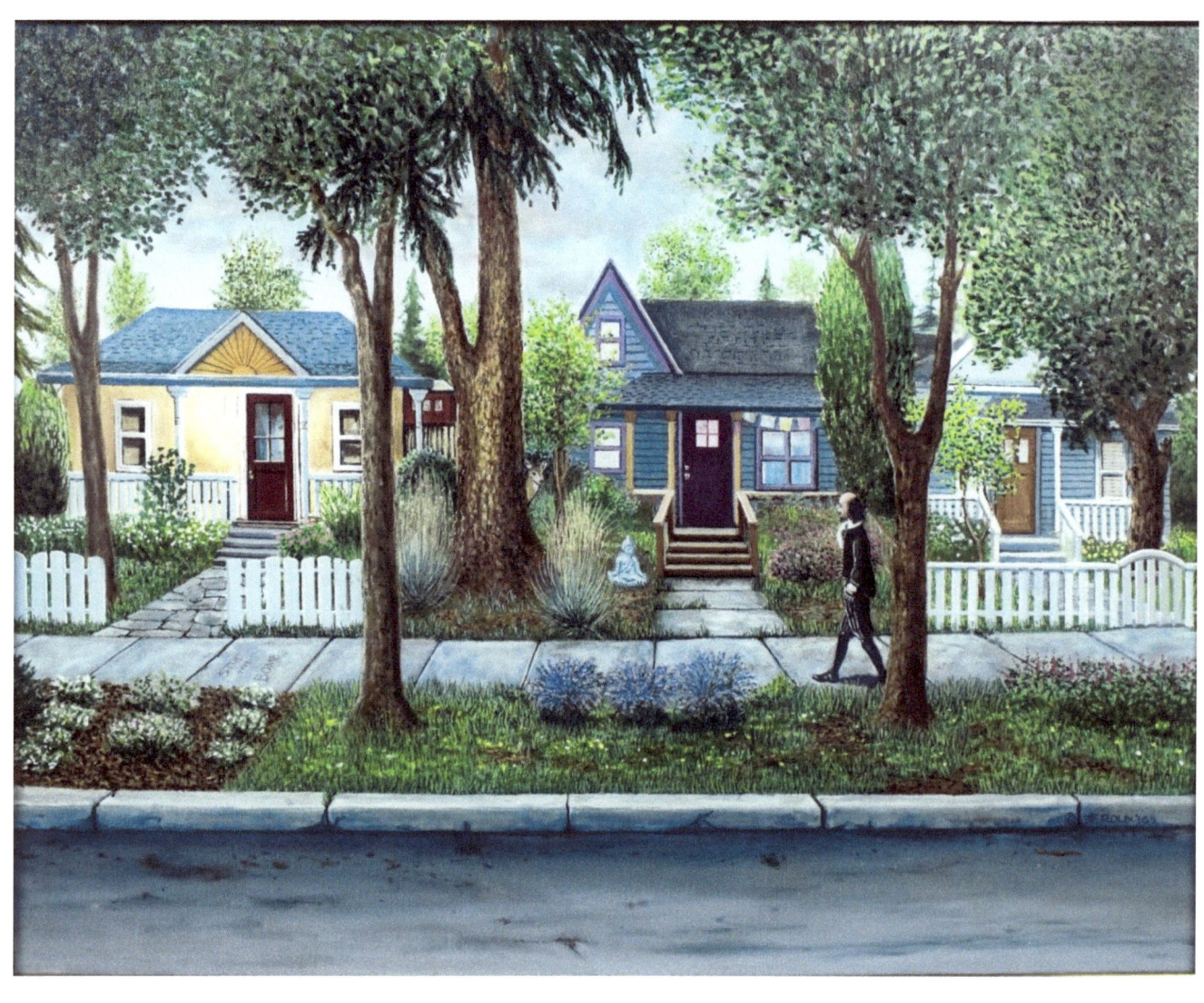

"Railroad District Constitutional"

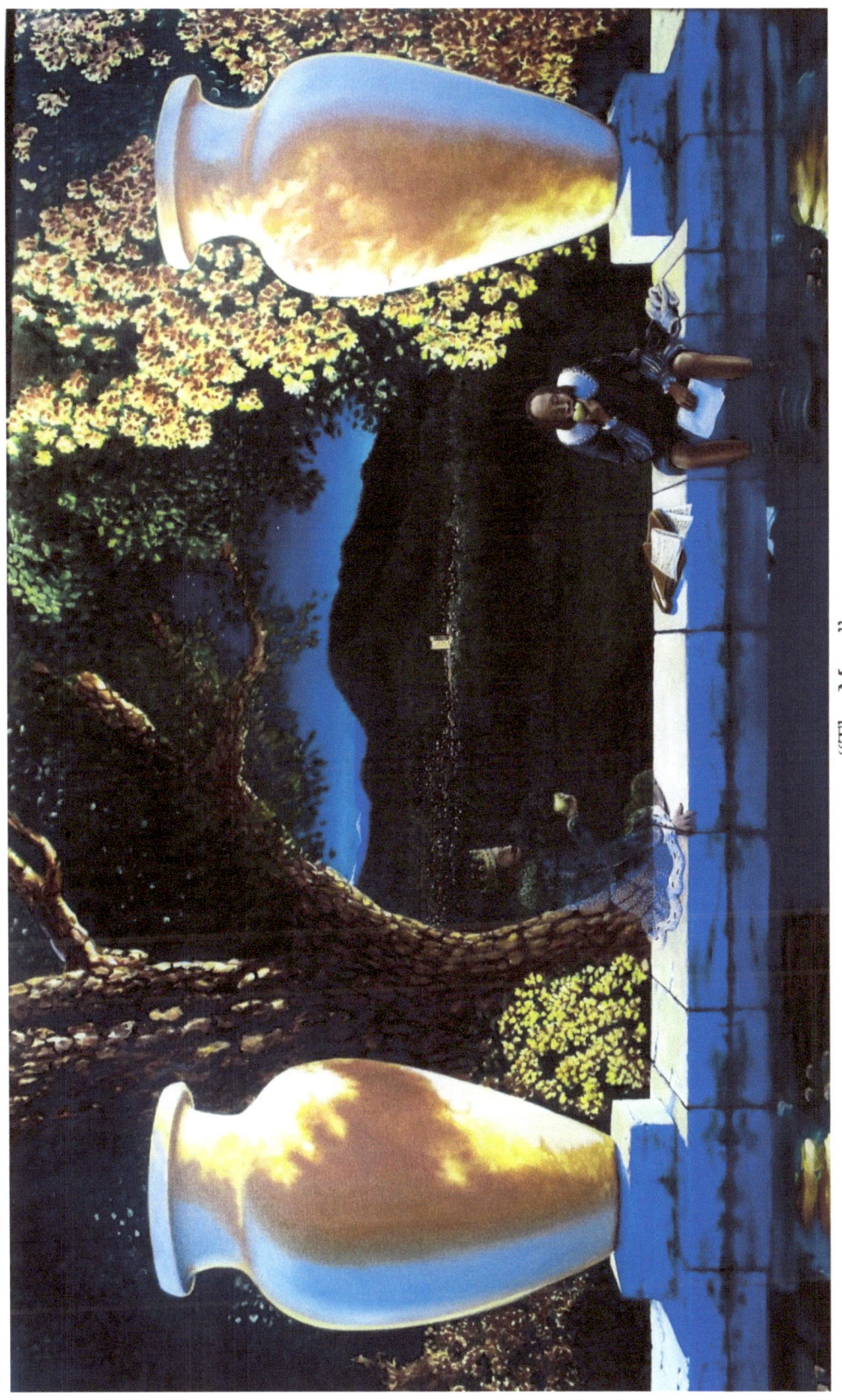

"The Muse"

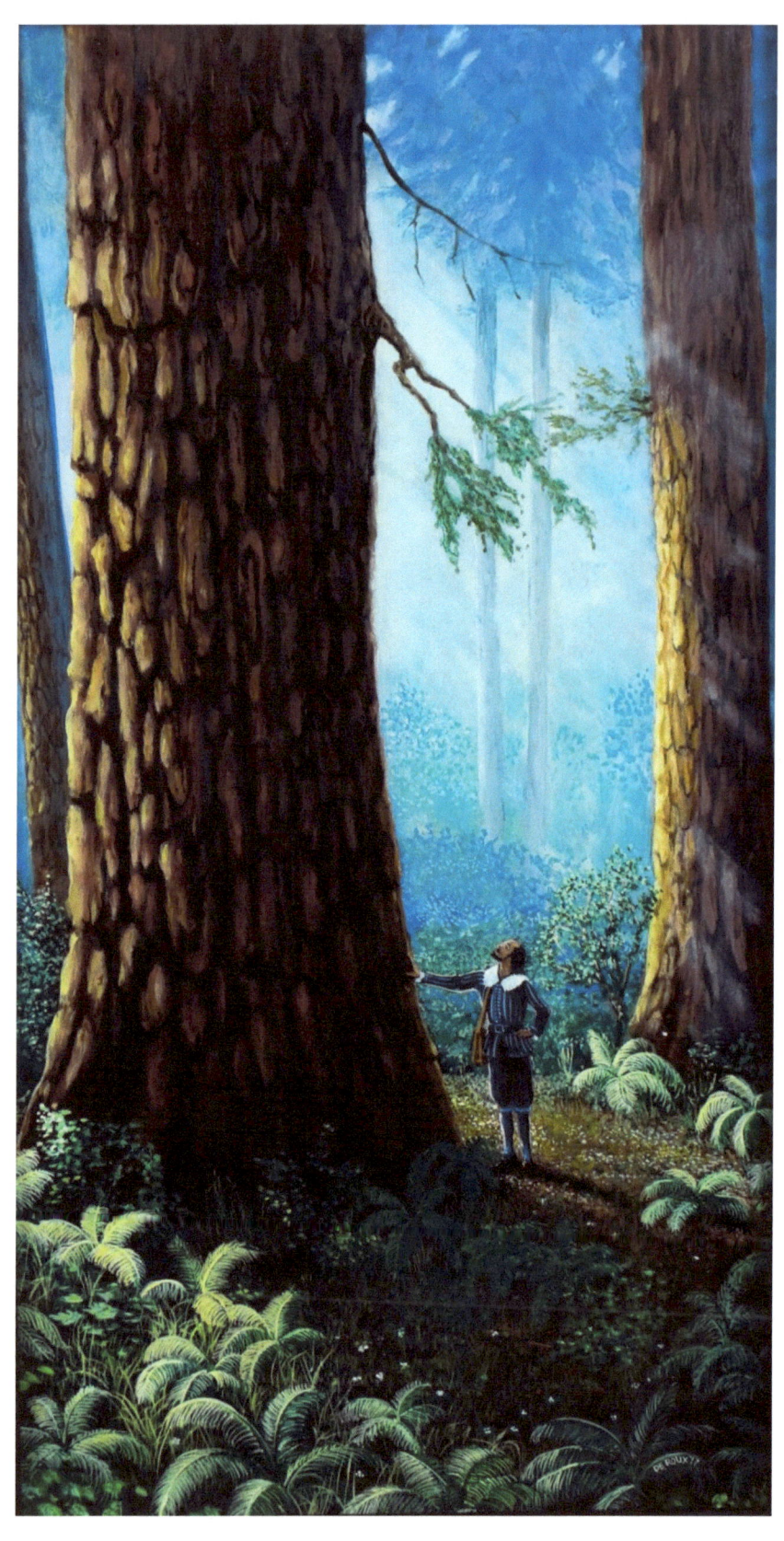

"Redwoods"

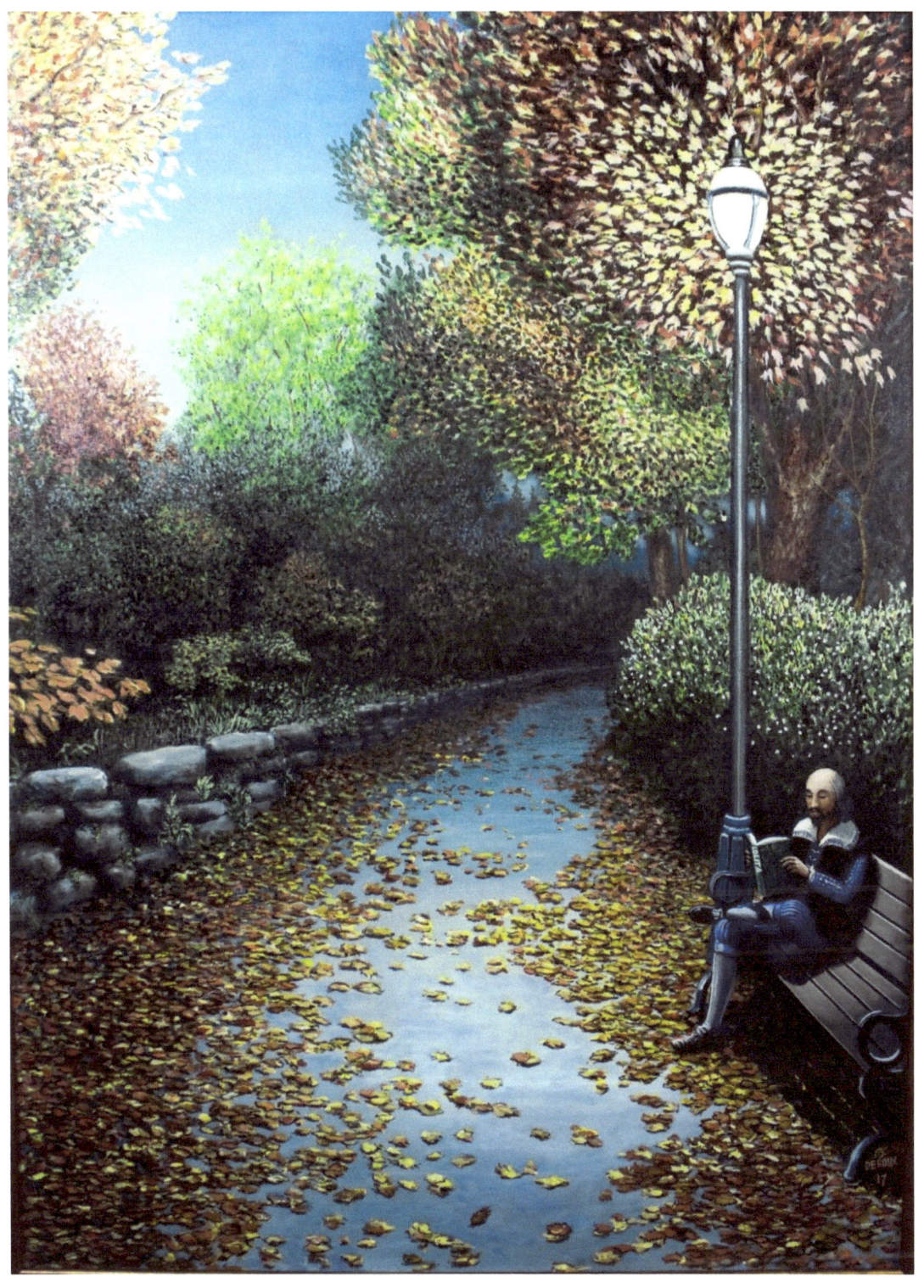

"In the Park in the Dark"

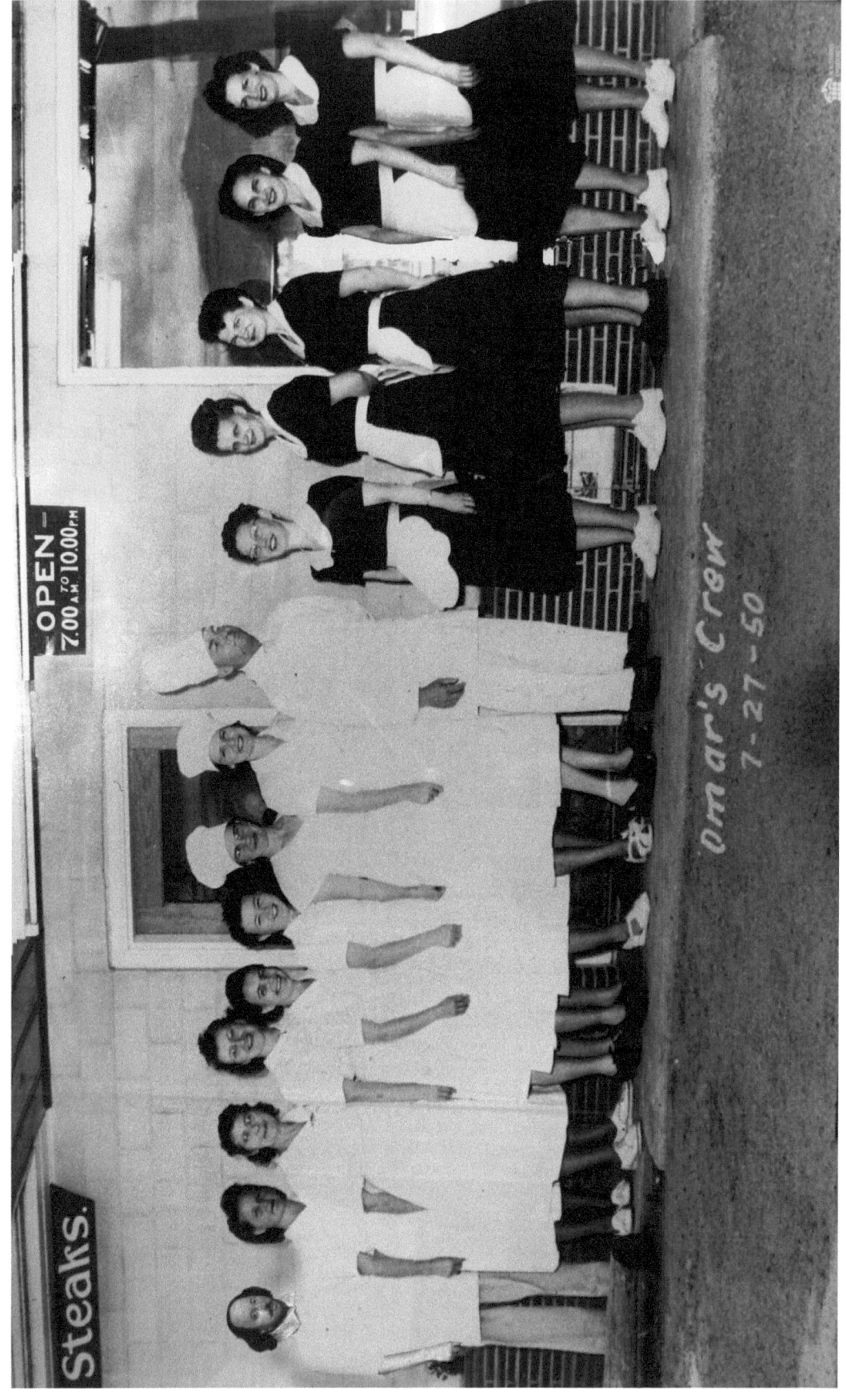

Staff photo "Omar's" Restaurant,, Ashland

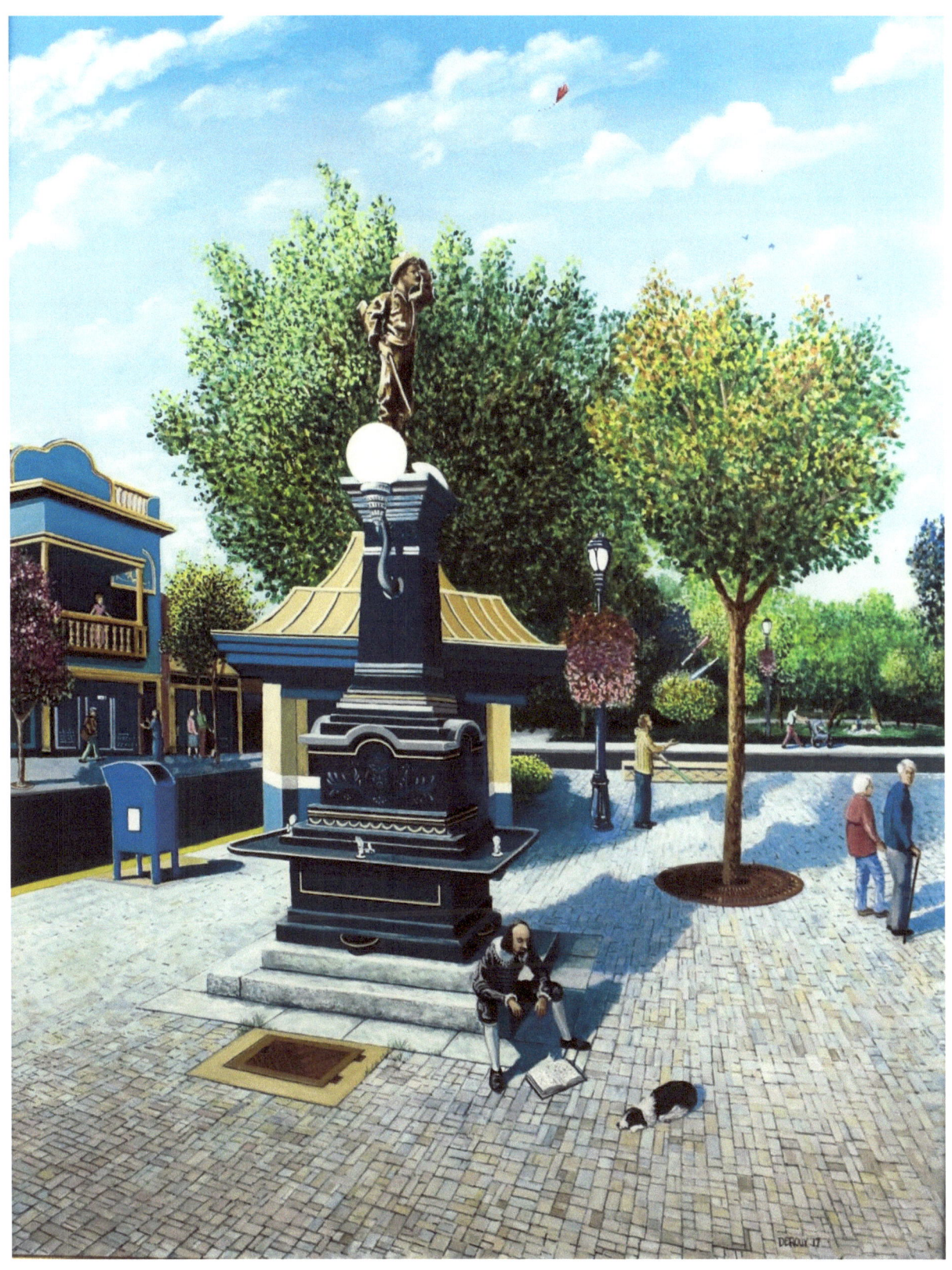

"Shakespeare on the Plaza with his Dog Lithia"

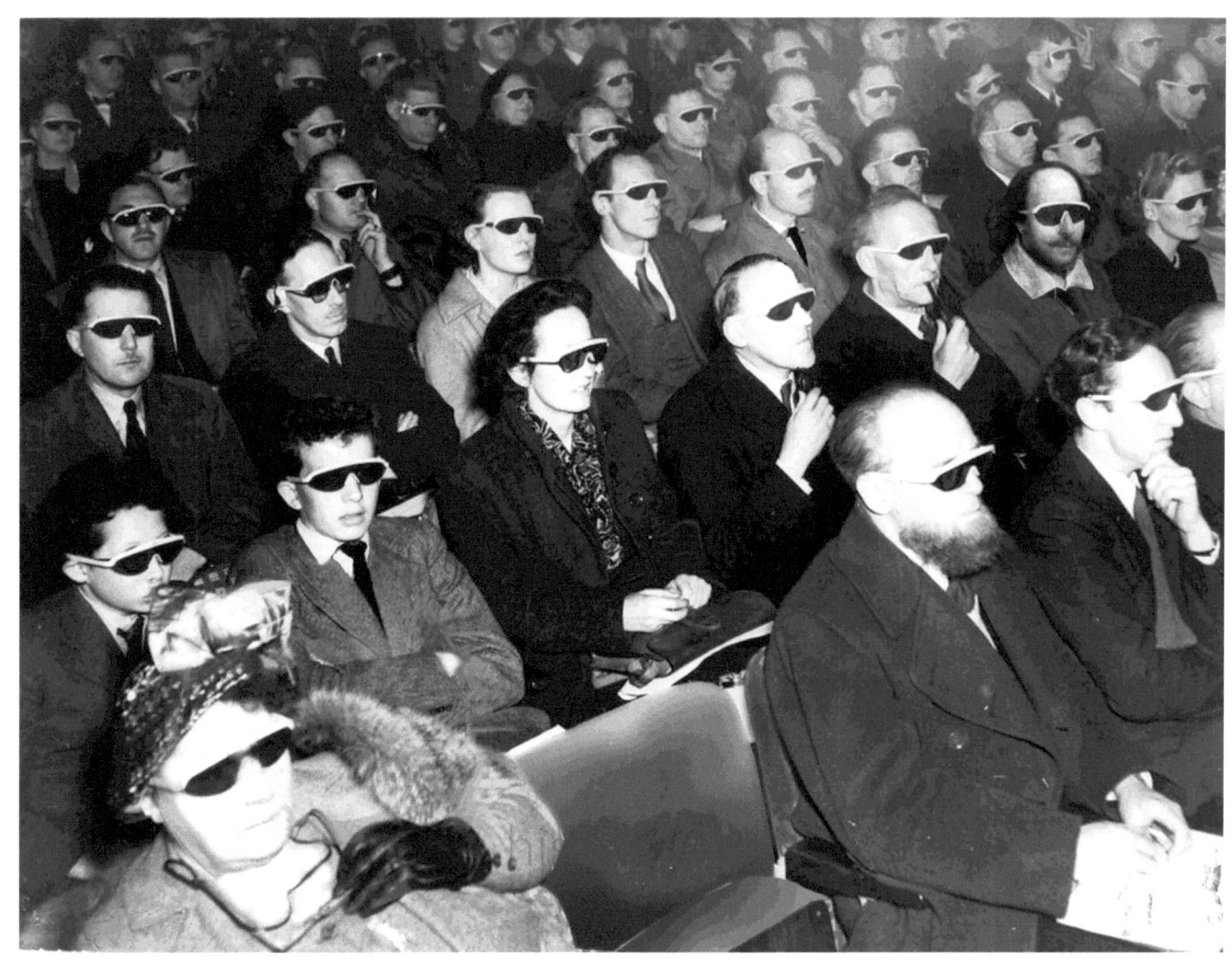

"Got Theater?"

This photograph cannot be verified as being that of
Shakespeare due to the fact you can't see his eyes.
Also, I don't know what theater it is taken in,
but I date it around early 1950s New York City because
he is sitting next to Marcel Duchamp (with pipe).
This picture shouldn't probably even be in this book.
But if it really is a picture of him, then, yes it should
definitely be in the book, even though it's not in Oregon.

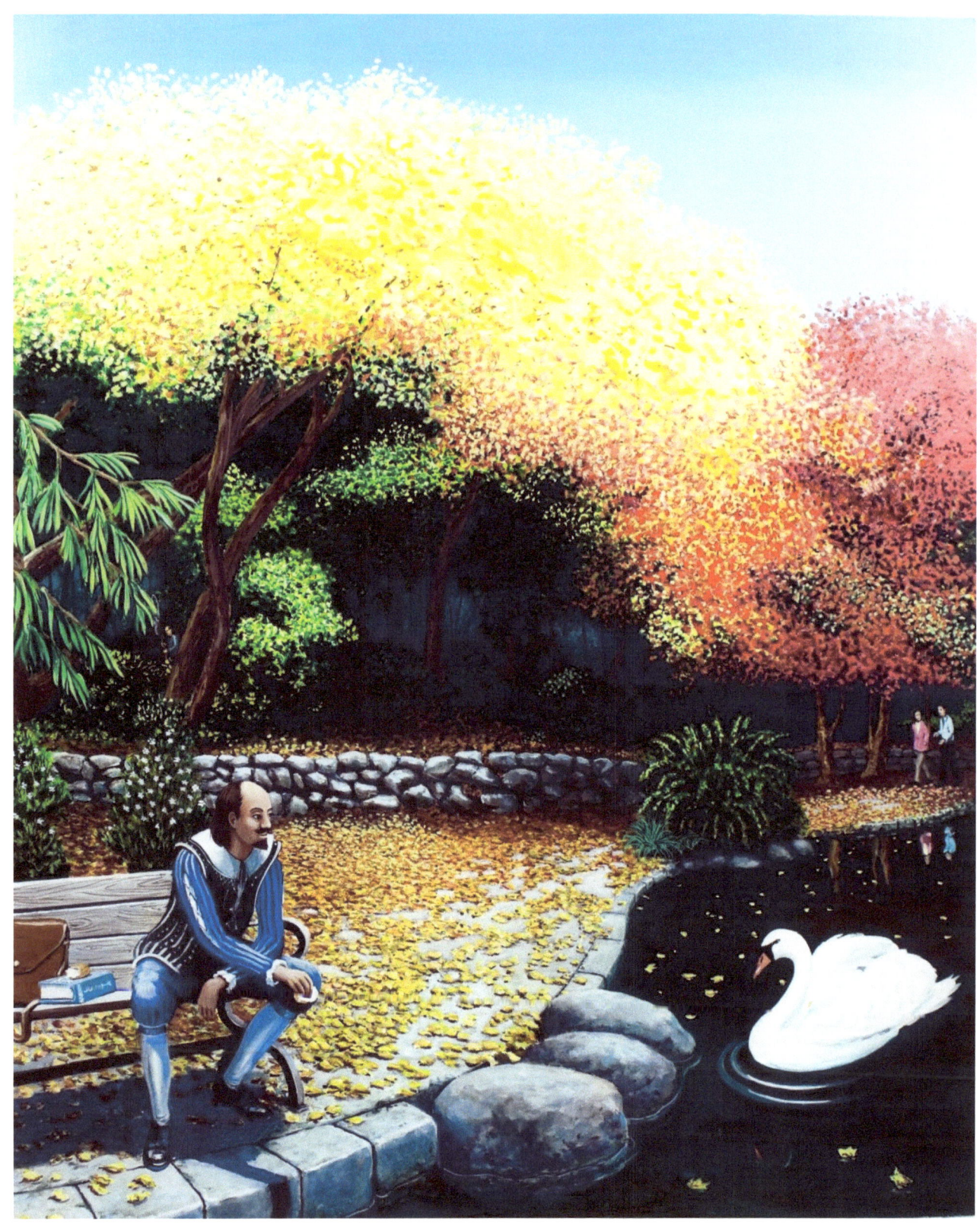

Nabokov's Quest

The famous Russian writer Vladimir Nabokov
lived in Ashland in the mid-fifties during which
time he finished his masterpiece "Lolita".
He is seen here, back in the bushes, indulging in
one of his other obsessions:
lepidoptery.

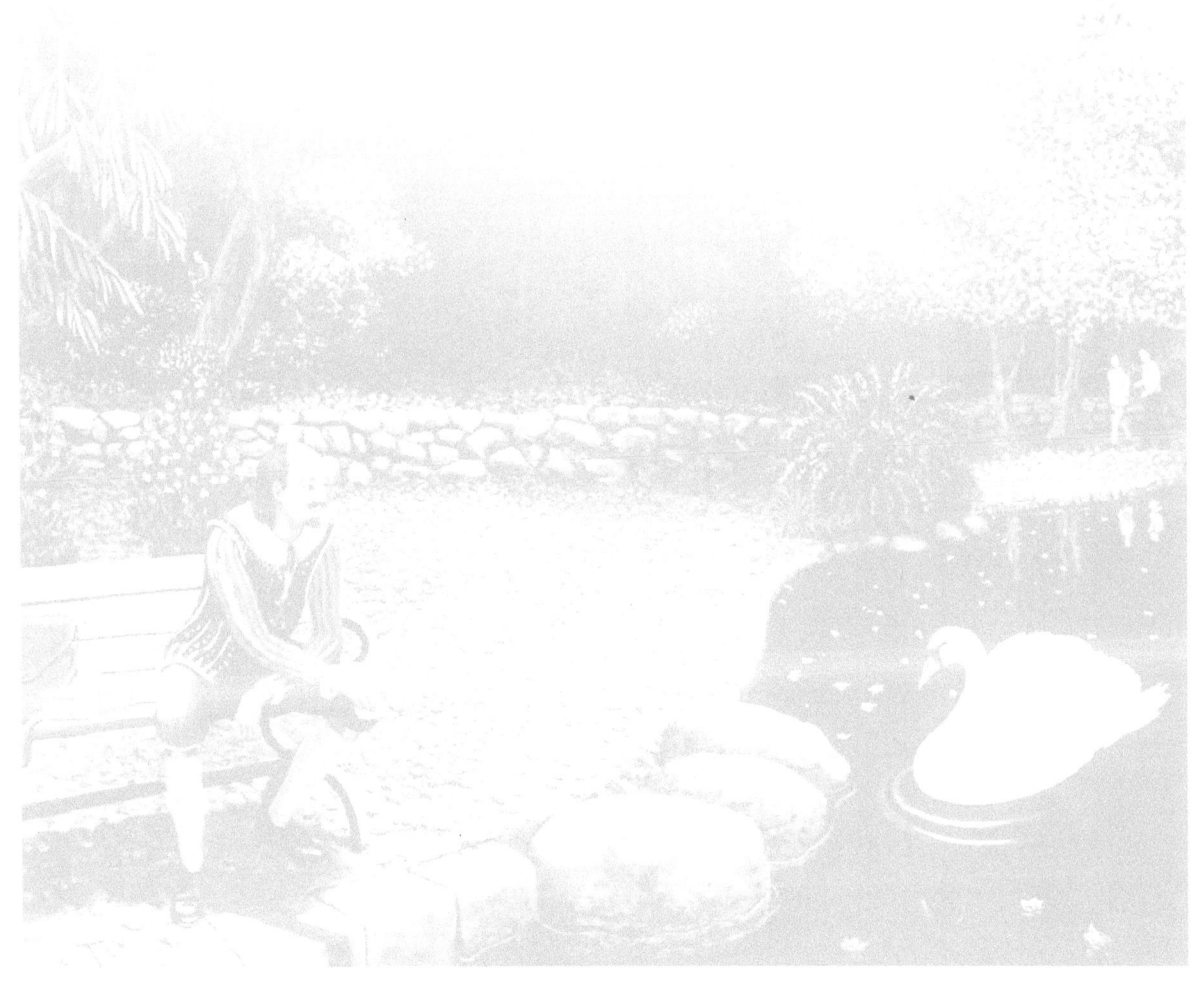

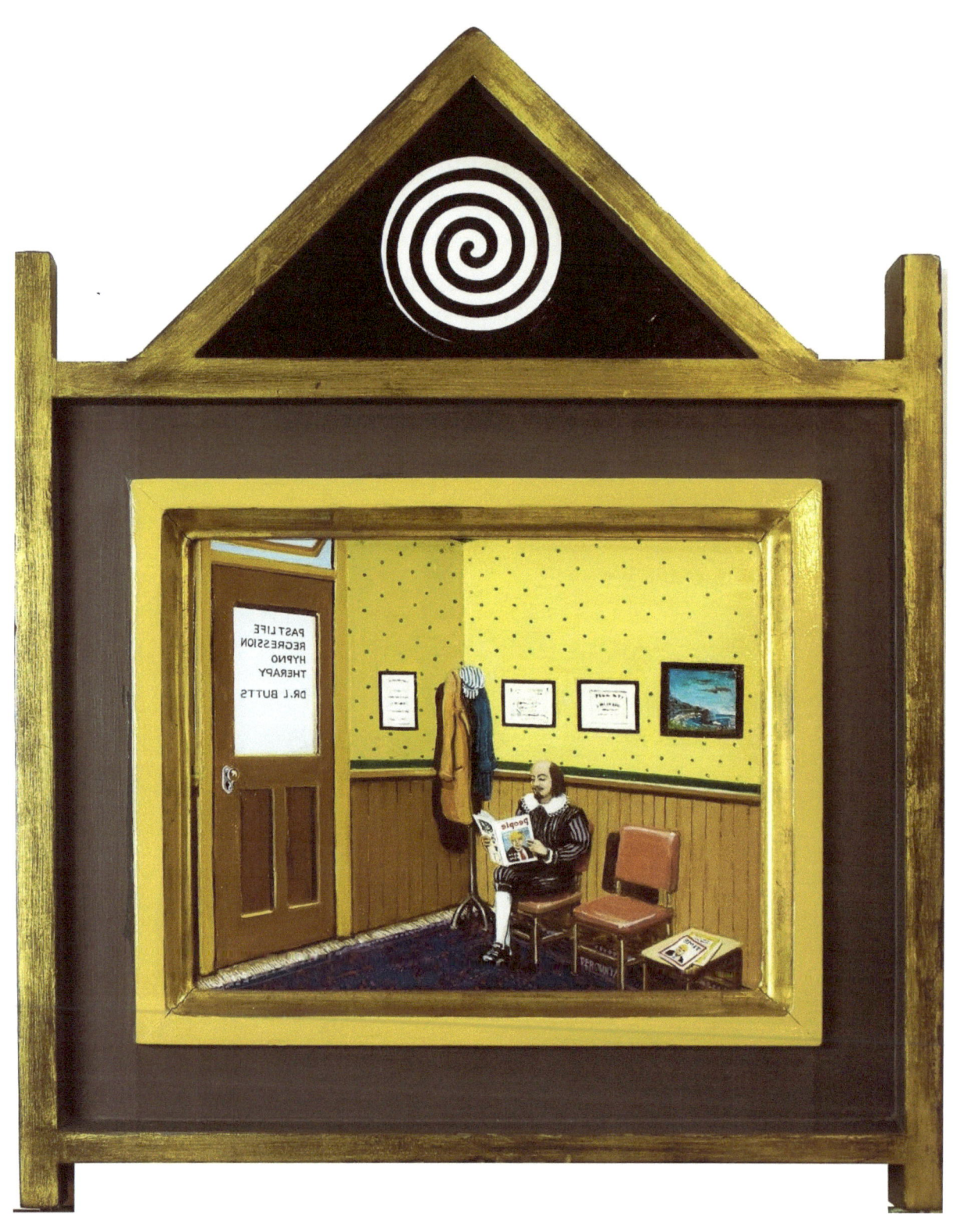

"At the Therapist's Office"

A survey of Ashland businesses reveals
counselors and therapists of all sorts.
Life architects and zen masters abound....
explorers of the inner universe longing to reveal their
secret knowledge to those seeking answers
to their mysteries...longing to live.

They all have patience. This one is sitting in the waiting
room, or more likely, waiting in the sitting room.

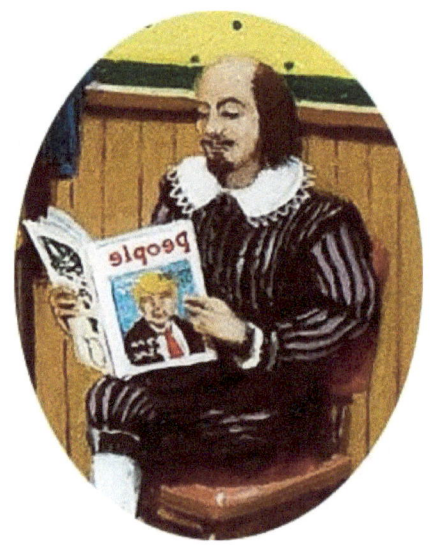

Some people say I didn't write this book…
That the book wrote itself.

Well, I wrote this book.

End of story.

Thank you .